Shades of Life

Donna Morgan

BookLeaf Publishing

India | USA | UK

Presentation by *BookLeaf Publishing*

Web: www.bookleafpub.com

E-mail: info@bookleafpub.com

ISBN:9789358314304

First edition 2024

DEDICATION

For my soul sisters, you know who you are. You have helped guide and walk with me as I grow, heal and unlearn the tough aspects of life.

To my family for so much of my inspiration and joy as well as the lessons along the way.

To my Husband, my rock and my anchor, you keep me grounded with love and always being there when I need you.

To you all, I love you more than words can ever express.

ACKNOWLEDGEMENT

I acknowledge my own healing journey and the twists and turns it has taken me on.
Discovering my love of writing from a feeling place and my inner glimpses and awe of new aspects of me every step of the way.

I send love and acknowledge all of you who will read these words, may they help you grow and discover aspects of yourself too.

PREFACE

Discovering the pearls and gold through the
darkest journeys to the highest highs.

This is shades of a healing journey in life.

Life's storm

Life's storm

It rages and swirls It's never relenting

Never ceasing its battering waves

Eroding your edges night and day

The storm clouds writhe

Intensity rises, boiling and bubbling, sucking out
all light

Freezing shut, your lungs
Your ability to see

Shades of dark all around never allowing the
light to ground

The sun shines outside

Bird songs continue

Yet the inner storm is a raging foaming beast
A terror thing, never allowing a moment's peace
A horror so enormous you are lost within
Squeezing and hiding you pushing into the
deepest darks of the fear

The ground, a thing felt under your feet
Yet not felt for the unseen storms raging breath

A feeling so intense, you cannot breathe

Stop!

Cease

Calm

So I may breathe and feel a seed of worthwhile

But it doesn't stop
It never stops, it batters on
Like the white squall storms

For days and nights, the feelings run
Fear and unworthiness, the drivers this time
Hate and the pain for a thing said that can't be
undone

A constant feeling of causing others pain,
A constant reminder again and again.

I said a thing
I created this pain; I am no good

I am no name

I am shame and doubt
Filled with despair

Lashed with anxiety
I do not belong here; I do not belong, a waste of
space that all went wrong

The feelings ebb, a small slip but the intensity
rises

There it is, a glitch
What is it I feel I don't know I can't feel

I don't know after so long how to feel
Numbness drives me

There is no feeling it is real

The storm is battering me with every breath
Growing and boiling a writhing mess

Let me breathe, please let me breathe

Let me see as clearly as need be
Let the comfort of reality come back to me.

Let me feel
Let me be free.

Sit and Be

Sit

Be

Sit in silence

Let it be

Feel the silence

Feel yourself breathe a sigh into the air

Hear the birds speak

As the air whispers your name

See the colours of nature

As you soften your spine to gaze

The colours of life surround you now

Every moment of life belongs to the now

Feel your lifeforce

Let it speak your song

Let yourself drift in the rhythm

As you meander and hum

You know you are alive?

Do you feel it in your heart?

But do you feel your body?

Or just your mind

Do you shun the silence?

Because you might unwind

Do you stuff it all down with the overindulgence
of life?

Or do you bury your head in the sand to hide?

Living undercovers where the darkness lets you
reside

Do you know your own energy?

Your soul

Your lifeforce

Do you overspend your energy?

And never renourish in positive ways

Do you listen to your body?

Or does your mind drive every day?

Are you afraid to sit and be with yourself?

With no electronic stimulation

Only with nature and yourself

Are you so disconnected and won't let the
silence in?

Do you tell yourself you're too busy?

Doing the thing

Let it in

Let it in

It's not scary at all

In the silence, you will let yourself in

You will feel the air in your body

Your breath as you breathe

Your heart beating rhythmically

You will begin to let it all be

You will discover under it all

That you are a compassionate heart beating

Not just a mind after all

So now do you see?

When you sit in silence

And let it all be

You will begin to breathe

Sit and Be

Life cycle

Life
It comes and goes
Fast or slow
It speeds up
Slows down
It never stops
Evolving all around
It's too short
Or too long
Too old or too young
It never stops but continues on
Years and generations from a single couple
Does it stop?
Will it end?
Evolution says no
Life continues to begin
It ends in a blink
A heartbeat stops
Another starts
It never stops
No matter how much strain there is
Unrest
Destruction
Conflict or gang wars
Life continues to be the miracle that is with us all.

Compassionate Heart

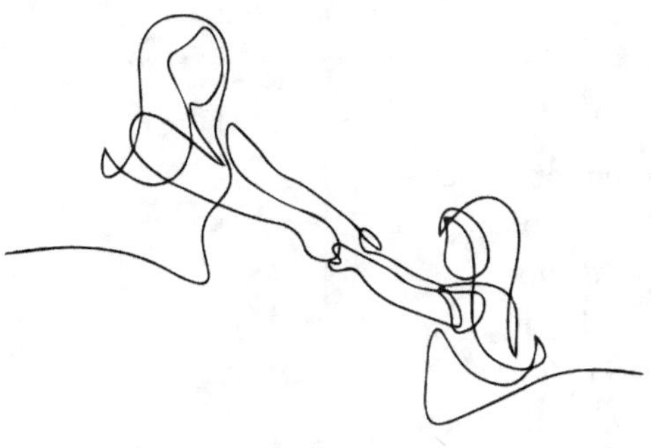

What is it you hold near and dear to your hearts?

Do you know?
Do you?
Do you care at all?

Is it something you do not want to share?

Is it a secret?
Hidden deep in your sacred treasure chest

Do you want to share or fear the worst
If you share you might be ridiculed
Laughed at or worse

What if all it took was a spark
A glimmer of love

Compassion for your heart and everything you
hold close

What if sharing that one little spark created a
wave
For others to open their hearts
Creating more waves of love and compassionate
hearts
Creating the joy to start a revolution of the
hearts

What a gift that would be
A gift of the tender brave heart

The gift of love is the place to start

Open your heart and hold compassion to see
The sacred treasure that is hiding near and dear
to your heart

Let others begin to see.

Creative Creature

Creative creatures of the night

Where are you hiding?

What corner of the night do you sit in?

What is it about the magic of night?

That brings you alive.

Dancing your words across the lines of each
page.

Flowing freely with shapes and spines.

Inspiration rising

Sparks ignite.

Creative creatures come out from hiding.

Dancing wildly at the writing hour

Sparking lives with words to share.

Glowing wildly these shadowy whisps

Tugging you get up

Get out of bed

1.11 am You cannot sleep

We must work it's time to begin

Come

Come

Listen to our tales

Listen to us as we whisper and glow

Listen now before we let you go

Take up your tools,

Your electronics

Your pencils to draw

Listen and write without any care.

Take it in
Write it down

Draw it alive

Bring it out!

Transform the magic of the night

Leap into the cosmic creative stream

Quickly, before it moves on.

The storytelling creatures of the night

The shadowy wisps.

Swim past, fly high and move fast

They land alive and loose

To those who answer the tugging night call

Fear them not

Embrace them now

They are the muses of a magical Creative life.

Who Am I?

Who is that being?

Who is the one that stays hidden?

Not seen

Who is she that hides from life?

Who is she that continues to hide?

Why do I hide?

From what I know not

Staying invisible

Not good enough for this life

Stories flow

The mind chatter starts

Numbness sets in

The blocks are not separate or apart

Protection mechanisms bind the heart

The hidden self is never free in this life

The hidden self, afraid all the time

Who is the hidden person within?

Who would I be if the spell breaks?

And I live?

How can this hidden self come out of the dark?

To be seen and heard

To create with a joyful spark.

Living in the Shallows

Staying in the shallows,

Playing it safe,

Living in the safety of this clear foreseeable space,

Not venturing further than the depth of my waist.

Not swimming in the deep it's a far too dangerous a place,

Stay away from the predators and the unseen things of the deep.

Circle and hunt waiting to pounce or kill.

To rip you apart and leave you misshapen and
strewn.

Dark things live in the depths far safer to stay in
the shallows.

Nothing will get me if I stay in a safe space.
But how do I grow if I don't venture into the
deep?

What of the sharks that swim beneath the
surface?

How do I learn if I stay in the escape place?

What will I miss if I don't swim to the depths?

What will I lose if I stay in the shallows of life?

Ebb and Flow

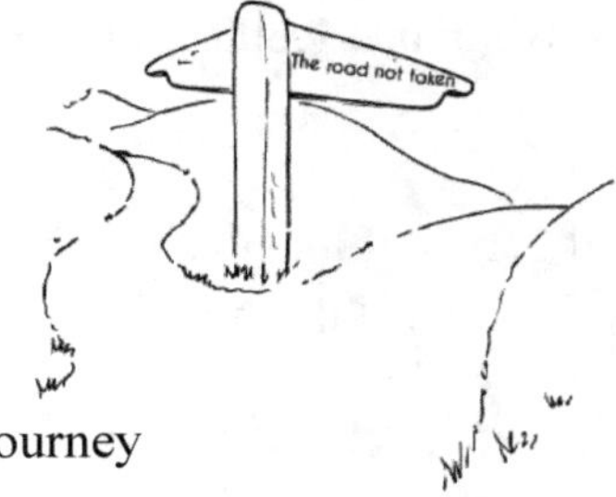

Life is a journey

A tide that ebbs and flows

It crisscrosses pathways

With or against the flow

It flows into life

It retreats away

It ebbs into being

When flow shouldn't be

We journey a path

We fight the flow

Embracing the ebb

Not believing we are ready to receive

A bountiful life

This is life for we are human after all

It is our existence

It is also our downfall

Embrace the flow

Celebrate the Ebb

Look all around you

Let your flow begin

No longer will you crisscross the paths.

But follow a flow that is just right for your heart.

Running

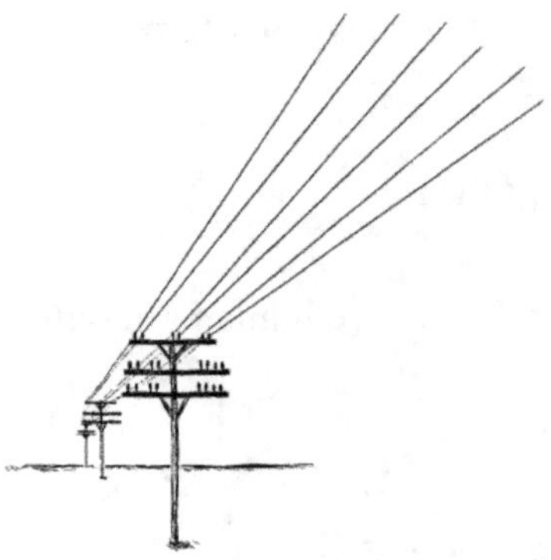

Seeing the road
Feeling the steps
One by one
The jolt of my foot hitting the ground
Bump again as my other foot falls
Thump as my foot hits the pavement once more
Running
Always running
Never slowing down
How is it that I feel every step and sound
Why am I running?
I do not know
It's easier than sitting still
It's easier than to face the fall
Not knowing how to process life
Not knowing what to trust and believe this time
Holding on, breathing hard

Running along the river's facade
The water is a constant calming place
Breathing heavily
Pick up the pace
Running is the way for me
Running is the key to sanity.
As I sit here in this feeling state I'm running,
running trying to escape

Dark Shadow Me

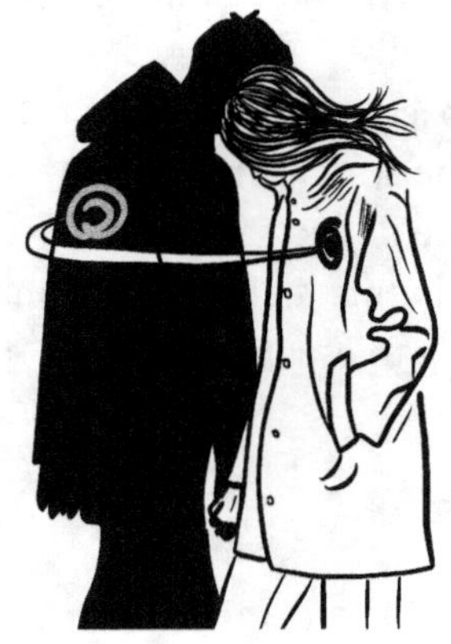

I cannot see
I cannot see
The darkest shadows envelop me

The night is the worst
It creeps about and slides
Its tendrils are like smoke
All around the walls of time

It does not hide
Creeping through the room in shadowy waves
Cracking me open again and again

Releasing the fears and the wraiths of the night
Unhinging and re-engaging the unforgiving
terrors of the heart
Opening old wounds once again

Feeling words that vibrate deep in the shell of
my skin

Whispers kisses so gentle and soft
Many nights I feel the harsh kiss of the night
It's a roller coaster ride of quitting, giving up

A slide deep into an abyss of no light
A sea of emotions that buffet all over the place

Feeling ever alone

Never good enough to be at home
Delving deep into the dark shadow of unworth
Not knowing how to shift it all
Not knowing if I want to

Now as the darkness calls
I slide deeper into the arms and the folds
The tides roll over me again and again
Rolling out and affecting those close to my skin

But how?
How can that be?
How is this affecting anyone but me?

I cannot see
I cannot see

I cannot see

Past the deep shadows that haunt my peace
They haunt me

Do I care?

Maybe a little
I just want it to go away
I want the whispers and the pain to sink into the
blackness and fade deeply and forever away
Taking me with it so I can hide away from eyes
Letting me find a new disguise

The darkness is relentless
It comes and comes
It always there
It never stops
It is a companion
It is a soft comfort of feeling alone and unloved
It is the world that feels harsh
Uncaring
Unjust
But is this real or just a lie?

Is it the darkness whispering so many lies?
Or is it really a deep dark place that holds us to
hide

Not allowing ourselves to see the truth of the
wall
Never unlocking the safety chest
Oh please don't let me fall

The Facade

What is this I see
Smooth and beautiful
A gem
A jewel
A stone of beauty and worth
Is it me?
Yet it is a façade
A shell polished up for value and to shine
The shell is thin
A veneer of life
Behind the shell hangs the corpse of the night
The foetal skeleton is it alive?
Is it real?
Is this a cocoon to hold me in?
Is the cocoon to keep me from feeling?
A full-size skeleton
Not looking or seeing
But in a stasis life
Is it a skeleton I cannot see?

For my view is clouded by the jewel to please
The jewel, the colour of turquoise clouds in the
sea
The colour of Larimar the smoothness so
beautiful it bares to be held
Yet the cocoon sleeps in a foetal space
Waiting for the day to arrive
Alive in its own space
The day its value will truly be held
The value of the life that lives within the façade
The value of self
The worthiness waiting to unfold
Living not breathing
Sleeping but awake
The cocoon hangs

It waits

Waiting for what
What needs to be
Waiting for the leaves to sprout on the tree
Waiting for recognition
For the signs of a valued life
The worthiness signs
Are they rich and awake
Fear
Panic
The anxiety unfolds
The skeleton shudders and curls up even more

The process begins to open
Unfold
Slowly the skeleton begins to uncurl
A knee sticking out
An elbow
A toe
The shoulders relax let it all go
How, when where, and why has this happened?
I don't know
Why am I not afraid to fall?
Why is my value so fearful of life?

The fear is the cocoon to keep it safe and alive
Gently protected so it may survive
The unfurling begins with a shudder of life
The cocoon opens
The stone cracks
She is really alive
The value is not surface-deep
The truth of her value runs cell-deep
Her veins awaken and become flushed, with the
warm milk of life
Her flesh grows upon her bones
She plumps out with glowing life
She begins to uncurl and takes a breath of love
She breathes and feels her essence flow
Her value, unmeasured this time
She has no benchmark for her Self worth
She is fresh and new and ready for life

A valued moment in this awakened time
Her worthiness is worth it and so is she
She is worth every moment of this life and the
breath she breathes
Her life has been long, her human decades,
many
She is worth all of it and more
She is worth the family, the business, the clients,
the love
She is worth the abundance, the wealth, and the
money too
She has value to offer
She is worth her space in this world
She is worth the self-love she knows she holds
Now more than ever she is feeling worth's flow
Her words so potent they awaken others
Helping them to grow
Never doubt or distrust
By following the strange things you feel
If you see your façade, go beneath
Feel to be real
Let your light shine let it all be seen
You are worth it
You are here
You are real!
Let your chrysalis emerge
Spread your beauty and be alive.
Stand in your true face
And Shine!

Flush of Acceptance

Peaceful
Calm
Blissful
Will it last?
Will it end?
Will the chaos and turmoil return once more?
This time feels different
Something shifts
Whispers
Let go!
Let go!
This time Chaos is not running your life
Peace felt
A grounding peace,
A subtle feeling
Acceptance
A subtle flash of life renewed
A deeper remembering
Positive feel
Sitting in the moment
Sitting in self
Not chasing shadows
Not holding on to the dark
But letting go
Being in the embrace

A healthy stream
Acceptance of all
Connecting to self
Feeling the first flush
Let's go!

Stumble or Fall?

Listen, Listen, to the feels of life

Listen

Listen
To a moment in time

Feel it
Feel it

Feel it all
Who cares if you stumble

You won't succeed if you don't fall
And fall you will
It's part of the plan

But the beauty is in getting up
Recovering and doing it again

Doing it differently
Doing it without shame
Doing it without the care of blame

Do what you must

But know the lesson you choose
Is your choice

It's wise to let go
The feelings, the moments, the distractions, the
pain

It's wise to feel, feel and feel again
Feel it all

Do it with intention, joy and trust

Who cares if you stumble
And let yourself fall

You are the keeper of those moments in time
You are the one who lays blame and does not
shine
You are the reason you feel

You are the reason for choice.
You are real.

Treasure Seek

Searching Searching
Praying
Asking
Where are the answers
Never found
Looking everywhere
Looking outside
Asking others
Never seeing, at all
Looking to others will bring you undone
Looking within
No
No
Never
Not at all

Don't look at the treasure you have hidden well
Don't ask yourself
Let it fall
The answers aren't hidden
They are shrouded in life
Find what you seek
Find your face in the light
But hide you do
From the questions you seek
It's easier to be outside of yourself
Than to have your own counsel to keep
Seek out the treasure
It's yours after all
Seek out your answers
Don't let yourself fall

Confusion

Challenging
Seeing
Believing
The lies
The stories of generations
The tales that twist with time
Beliefs buried deep
Living under your skin
Living within you
You don't know where to begin
You challenge the inner conflicts
You weep with despair
You feel those moments
Deeply ingrained in time
You question and question
You find the thread to unwind

Slowly and steadily you shift and know
Something is changing
Your outer world tells you so
In the blink of a moment
A nanosecond in time
The confusion starts
How
What
Where?
Why?
In that precious moment
You begin to unwind
The stories and beliefs of lifetimes
Confused
You rejoice
It's all part of the shift
It is you rewriting the new pathways
To new ways of life.

Footprints of life

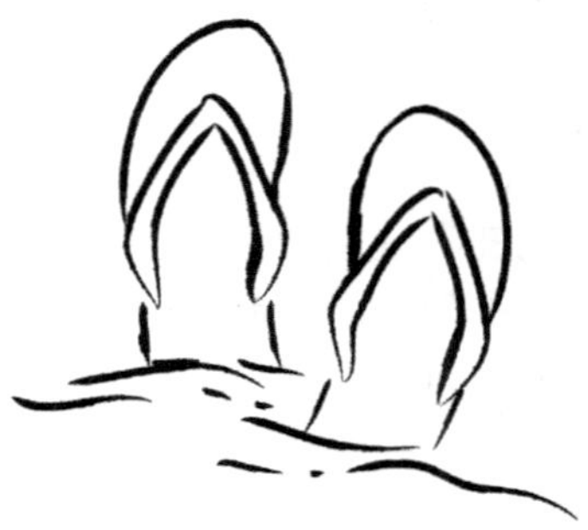

Ways of living
Travelling a life
How do you do this
What roads do you take
What paths along the route
Do you follow
Do you meander off on your own way to
nowhere
Do you have laser sight and always follow a
straight line
Do you stop and start taking time
Do you rush and hurry never seeing life
Do you follow your heart
Do you follow a map
Do you have guidelines from a book perhaps
Do you have a long-term plan ahead
Or do you play it all by the seat of your pants
Are you adventurous
Or are you blind

Are you too scared to stop and decide
Are you here and there, to and fro
Or are you organised on the go?
Do you reach a destination and never see the
journey you took?
Or do you see the journey and all of its flow
Are you aware of your footsteps
And how you tread life
Or do you care not for the journey of life
Only seeing your destination as the end of your
life

Do I fit?

Where do I fit?

Do I fit?

Where do I belong?

Feeling like a square peg in a tight-fitting round hole

Deep within an inner chamber, the darkness sits

Biding its time to fracture and blip

This time the enormity of not fitting in

Feeling the greatest need for approval

Acceptance and approval from where and when

A high five or some deep loving care

Is it all a lie?

Electric shock pulse shooting through me

Is it a charge ready to ignite?

Or a shock to shutdown

Not wanting to illuminate deeper darker space

Keeping it distant locked away in the inner
abyss

This gnawing un-acceptance and non-approval
quest

For not fitting in

But trying to be a clone

Not being the pretty one, the petite, the shiny
showpiece

The intelligent one, the one with a career or
degree

Being too sensitive

Too emotional to bare

Too moody or tearful, a sook, get away from
here

Hide the tears from parental eyes
Not good enough from the first moment's page
of this life

Not the Princess born

But the ugly duckling that never grew to be a
swan

The big lump of coal that no one wants to own

Not the prize catch, but second best every time

Always at the back invisible from sight

The one who isn't right for this life

No space is mine in this displaced life

All the feelings bubble up inside.

All the ways of not being good enough to belong
each day

Not acceptable for gifts

Not acknowledged each year

Celebrations of life a non-event every time
Not acceptable to the self

How can that be?

Many lives in one

Many lives I see

Many faces presenting

Do they stand out at all

It meets at a point to undermine the power I feel

A life that feels so fraudulent and fake

Unreal is the sense that comes into my being

Every illusion awakens as a snake from a deep
sleep

The serpent arises ready to strike you in your
sleep

Taking the poison to the deepest point of the
unknown

Killing beliefs

Once again they are toxic and harbouring in
your body now

Slipping into the truth occasionally now

Too afraid to show the power, strength and
courage you run

Hide!

Run!

Fearful of being loved

Too afraid to be seen

Too scared to let go

Fearful you will fall

You can't use your voice your jaw freezes shut

Fearful of death

Is this another life?

This can't be real, yet it feels true to the core

Does anyone truly care when you are hiding
curled up on the floor?

Breathing deeply with a sigh

Seeing the layers, it's time to let yourself silently
cry.

Radical Acceptance

Radical Acceptance
Radical changes in life
Radical ways to feel
From fear to love
That's new life
Let the moments be as they may this time
No
Accept what isn't
Not what you believe it needs to be
Accept that feeling of love in the shades
between
Feel your acceptance
Please don't push it away
Love it boldly
It's yours to claim
Feel those moments as you tread the inner path
Let your feelings rise

Follow your heart
Let yourself heal
Listen to your heart's voice
Hear your body
Let her speak
You are the creator of your healing path
When you choose love over fear you cannot go
wrong
This is acceptance
This is the start
This is how you change reality
A world
A heart.
This is self-love
Let your trail-blazing ways show others how it's
done

Return to Grace

Return to grace
I feel you!
I feel you see your decomposed mummified
pieces lying within me
I'm sorry
Sorry I have not seen you before
Sorry I have kept you lying on the floor
Please forgive me for covering you up
For decades you were ignored till it took its toll
and you emaciated away
With no light to nourish you
Your life force drained
Now I see you
I feel your feather touch trying to awaken
I breathe
I breathe back into you sending you life
Nourishing your faded light

I watch you flesh out and begin to grow
As I sit and focus on you
I feel it is so
I feel I have forsaken you
Why
How
I do not know
But I feel a deep love a burning desire
To bring you back to being
To flesh you out with heart's desire
To fill you full of life's spark
To bring you to fullness
A brightness not felt for so long
Feeling you return home
To feel you speak
To allow this wonder to rise
To begin this new journey with life in my soul
You are my Grace my light my desires
I gently but fiercely allow you back to the spark
Plump with life
I feel you enter my cells, to grow
As I sit here I feel you begin to be fluid and melt
through my body once more
Creating the wholeness of who I am
I feel you!

Stages of Life

Phases of time

Childhood to motherhood

Motherhood to Maga

Maga to Crone

The Hag of Crones

The many landscapes we travel and traverse

The many states of being that are unseen but felt

We navigate the pathways as best we can

We listen and learn that's the way it's always
been

But what if the way we choose to move

Is different and strange to those that went before

What if we look at each phase of life as if we are
planting?

Seeding, growing, creating and harvesting it all

In the summer of our youth, we dream and plant
seeds

As maidens in the spring of our life, our seeds
begin to glow and ripen

As mothers, we create and move through our life

With the knowing that our creations will ripen
and grow

As we move forward in the seasons of life, we
enter our Autumn and our harvest begins

As Magas, we sit and ponder so much

How much have we missed out on in our youth?

Are we too old to be noticed anymore?

Are we indeed shunned for not being young at
all?

Too young to be old and too old to be young

Yet our mind, body and soul say different things

What is it that's changed in us at this time, we
are not young and full of seeds to plant any more

Yet we have many, many creations still to be
born

But time is not on our side

Are we even old enough to be wise?

Yet we are not yet the crone of old

We sit somewhere in the middle like a moonless
night

Somewhere in a landscape that is not talked of in
life

Then as we pass through this liminal land

We enter our Crone years and Winter has begun

We walk our crone for many cycles.

Until we meet our final stage the hag of crones

She is the one that the fables and myths speak of

Full of wit and feistiness, her no-nonsense
approach leaves her being hated and adored

She keeps her counsel and never breaks

She is the wisest of wise ones as she ripens and
bursts fully into her age

At winter's end, she leaves this place

With a long life lived she knows her fate

Navigating your life can be a journey tough or of
ease

Full of wonder and joy

Love, friendships and trials by the score

Many things challenge us on our journey of life

Many phases highlight our seasons of life

Yet none compare to the courage we have

When we decide to live our life and be the
person we are meant to be

You are free

You are free
Are you free?
You are free to be you,
Who do you wish to be?
With heart and soul
You find your divine spark
You follow your guidance
Your gut
Your instinct
Your heart

You know deep inside there is a spark
Let the stories go and find that divine heart
You have a choice
It is true
It is wise

It is your guidance
Feel it flow
Deep into being
Hear its voice
Believe what you are seeing
Bring it all together in a beautiful spark
Know you are free
Know your divine heart

Love your light

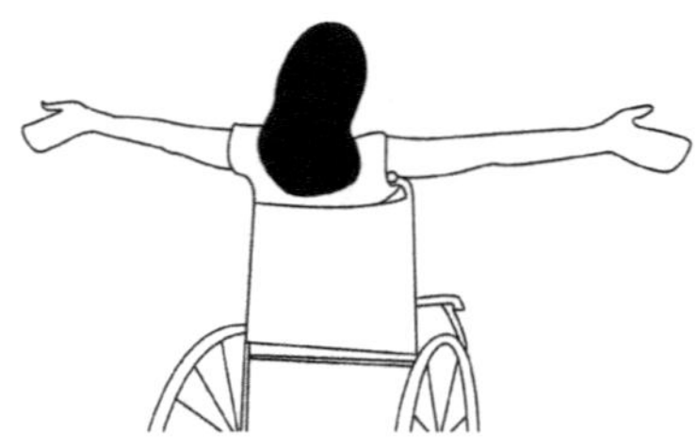

Fuel your heart
Fill it with love
Embrace the passion
Love your light
Hug your partner
Let them cry
Feel the nourishment within all life
Hold your lover gently tight
Feel the words
Let the whispers move
Passionately gently
Hold them safe too
Kiss them lightly
Like a whispered breath
Hold their hand don't let them slip
Let the love flow
Let your true feelings be felt
Create the heart space
The safe place for love
Create the loving essence and bring them home

Rage

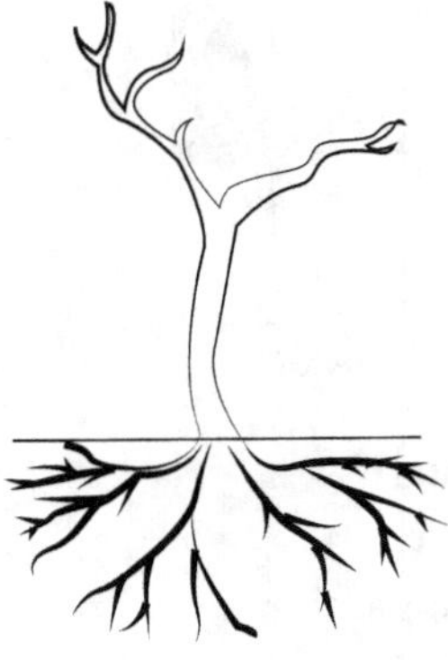

Raging storms
Seething and breathing
The oceans torrents

Rogue waves batter and destroy

Raging winds come to land
Tearing down cities
Destroying everything as she goes

So much water falling from the clouds

Get to high ground

The world begins flooding as oceans rise

Fire cleanses

Burning anything that hides

Rivers rise
Dams break

Streets become oceans
There is no escape

Blizzards happen
Destroying any view
Ice freezes over
Awaiting something new

Our earth buckles and heaves

Splitting open
Erupting homes

The angry heat spews out taking back what it
owns

So many ways to rage and roar
So much anger in nature's rational store

Do what you know in your heart of hearts to
help.

Don't ignore the calls
Don't give over to greed

Listen to nature's raging call.
Each place has its own unique spirit place
You just need to find it and reconnect to your
place

What is Life

Life what is it

I don't know
Is it even real?

Or are we plugged into non-reality

Is that our reality
Is it this earthly human space

Or

Is it a lie
Is unreal

This life that we live in.

I don't know

Is it even real?

Fear

Fears
Pain
Despair
Melting like butter in the hot summer sun
flowing like lava
The tide is strong
No stopping it now
It begins its overrun

Why does it
Why am I not normal
Why isn't this controlled

The feelings build up
Then they overflow

Fear
Pain
Despair
Once more

The shame rises
Shame of it all

Seeing this is all the same thing
It's all the fears of a lifetime gone
It's a view of the world from pain, shame and
fear
It's a view from the smallest moment in life
From the feelings of a time emotionally
undefined
The child is scared
The adult confused
Why this unnecessary action
This view

But the body doesn't lie
The motions rise

Fear
Pain
Despair
And now Shame
spark you this
How will others react again
The Shame of the moment
Enough to keep you home
Each time a reaction unfolds
A new level rises up
Til the day

You realise
You are a hermit living alone
The emotions flood
The reactions real

Hope and light
Disappear

Day dawned with a different view
A glimmer of hope and the inner child renewed
Miracles happen
Emotions calm
Nerves become unframed
Shame moves away
Fear is always a companion
Though now the light shines strong
Perspectives change
It's the view that creates the life you live

All my blessings for your Journey
Donna xx